Severn B

Disaster

25th October 1960

by
Chris Witts

River Severn Publications

Published by
RIVER SEVERN PUBLICATIONS
15 Riversley Road, Gloucester, GL2 0QU, England, UK
Website: www.severntales.co.uk
Email: chriswitts@hotmail.com
Tel: 01452 526202

Researched and Written
by
Chris Witts

ISBN 978-0-9532711-3-9

Re-printed 2011

Front cover:
From a drawing by Louise Bloomfield

Unless credited, all photographs are from the Author's collection
All endeavours have been made to trace the source of all other photographs used in this book.

Map which accompanied the Fire Service report
courtesy of Gloucestershire Fire & Rescue Service.

Acknowledgments:
*Susan Witts, The Citizen, Gloucestershire Record Office,
Gloucestershire Fire & Rescue Service, George Thompson,
Mike Meredith Edwards, The History Press, Fred Larkham,
and the BBC TV Inside Out West team*

Printed by:
Imprintdigital.net
Seychelles Farm, Upton Pyne, Exeter, EX5 5HY

Contents

Four Harker tanker barges lay on the mud at Shepperdine waiting for the tide. They were proceeding up the Severn Estuary, laden with petrol, bound for Sharpness, when thick fog descended on the river. The skippers felt it safe to lay here until the fog cleared on the next tide, not wanting a repeat of the disaster of the 25th October 1960.

SHELL STEELMAKER fully laden in Swansea Bay.

View from the wheelhouse of the WYESDALE H as she makes her way loaded up the Bristol Channel from Swansea.

WYESDALE H lying on the mud of the River Usk at Newport. She had discharged her cargo of petrol and now awaits the incoming tide to float off and return to Swansea for another cargo.

At times it could be quite frightening as these small craft ploughed through rough seas during a south westerly gale. No wonder there was a large turn over of lads, some only managed the trip to Swansea, then came back home by train!

Foreword

I left the Central Technical School for Boys in July 1960 at the age of sixteen with one ambition, to work on the tanker barges of John Harker Ltd as a deckhand. After a few weeks I was working on the *SHELL STEELMAKER,* then three weeks later I began working on the *WYESDALE H.*

It was all very strange to me, the long hours, being away from home and the hard physical work on deck. I will never forget that dreadful night of the 25th October 1960 but at the time I was so naive I did not realise the seriousness of what was happening. I remember the explosion and the huge ball of fire as the cargo of petrol and heavy oil ignited. After that we locked in safely at Sharpness and lay alongside the quay wall in the docks. I simply went to my cabin and turned in for the night.

Early next morning as we set off for Gloucester I can remember seeing the smouldering barges out in the Severn off Purton. As we travelled along the Gloucester & Sharpness Ship Canal, my parents were listening to the news on the radio at home. They immediately left to go down to Gloucester Docks and the first person they met was a lock-keeper at Gloucester Lock. He told them that all the crew of the *WYESDALE H* had been killed! Fortunately they soon learned that I was safe and would be back in Gloucester in a couple of hours.

A few months later as the vessel was in Gloucester Shipyard for repair, I heard a voice say to me, "Hey lad, I'm your new skipper". I groaned for it was none other than George Thompson, who had been skipper of the *ARKENDALE H* on that fateful night. I was in awe of him, in fact petrified! He and the new mate, Mike Edwards and I, worked together for several years and we had some great adventures together.

I would like to dedicate this book to George Thompson, who treated me like a son and changed me from a lad into a man. Also a big thanks to the mate, Mike Meredith Edwards, who taught me so much and indeed is still a good friend of mine.

The River Severn is classed as one of Britain's most dangerous rivers. Those who work on it respect it but sadly accidents still happen.

Chris Witts
Gloucester

July 2010

7

The *WASTDALE H* was built in 1951 by John Harker Ltd at Sharpness Shipyard. A sister vessel of the *WYESDALE H,* which had also been built in 1951 at Sharpness Shipyard.

The WASTDALE H in the drydock at Gloucester Shipyard undergoing her annual survey.

The WASTDALE H loaded with 351 tons of petrol leaves Avonmouth Lock.

The *ARKENDALE H* was built as a dumb tanker barge in 1937 by Richards Ironworks Ltd at Lowestoft. During 1948 this vessel was rebuilt as a motor tanker barge.

The ARKENDALE H at Lowestoft (left) shortly after being launched in 1937 and (right) at Gloucester as a motor tanker barge .

THE SEVERN BRIDGE DISASTER

Tuesday 25th October 1960

The shrill ring of the alarm clock quickly brought the young sixteen year old lad to his senses. It was 4am, an unearthly hour to be getting up but his tanker barge would be sailing from Monk Meadow Dock at Gloucester in a hour's time. There was no time for breakfast, just a quick wash before peddling furiously on his bike the four miles from his home in Gloucester to the docks.

Chris Witts, deckhand on the *Wyesdale H*, saw that the engineer was already on board with engine started and kettle boiling away on the galley stove. Making tea was the most important job for any deckhand in the John Harker fleet, as long as the skipper had his mug of tea in the wheelhouse he was happy. Yet today, Tuesday 25th October 1960, for the crew of the *Wyesdale H* it was not a happy day, in fact no day was pleasant, for this was a tanker barge with an unhappy crew.

This estuarial tanker barge was part of a large fleet of vessels, owned by John Harker Limited of Knottingley in Yorkshire, which carried oil products in their larger craft from as far as Swansea to Worcester and in the smaller tanker barges from Avonmouth to Stourport. The company had been trading on the Yorkshire waterways since the 19th century, then expanded to trade on other British rivers, the Severn included, where they came to in the late 1920's. Eventually they would have a large shipyard at Knottingley, where they built not only barges for their own fleet but vessels of all types for other customers, even a submarine during the Second World War. During the 1950's they began to build large tanker barges for the Severn area, carrying a cargo of 350 tons of oil and operating to all Bristol Channel ports and inland as far as Worcester.

The *Wyesdale H* was unhappy because the crew did not work well together. She had an old Yorkshireman for the skipper, a small dour chap, always seen wearing his trilby, not saying a lot to anyone. The mate, a young Gloucester man who, like the deckhand, just wanted a quiet life and did not say much either. Then there was the engineer, noisy, brash and certainly liked the sound of his voice. He would tell the mate and deckhand what to do, which upset the skipper, an argument would start and this would end with the two men fighting on deck! Finally the deckhand, (it was normal in the Harker fleet for the fourth hand to be a young lad), would be told to keep quiet and only speak when spoken to. If he did something wrong, he could expect a clip around the ear! For the deckhand on the *Wyesdale H* this was only his second week working on the vessel, in fact it was only his second month with the company. He had spent his first month on the *Shell Steelmaker*, a modern tanker barge with a five man crew, on charter to Harker's and operating in the same area.

The *Wyesdale H* may have been unhappy to work on but the vessel had superb accommodation, (a cabin each for the four man crew, a mess room and galley, plus toilet/washing facilities). Warm and cosy, the cabins were located at the stern end of the barge and built around the large engine room. She was part of the famous '*Dale*' fleet. In 1937 the company began naming all their vessels after the Yorkshire dales, with the suffix *H* and for every '*Dale*' vessel there was always a twin, the *Wyesdale H* being no exception, hers being the *Wastdale H*. Both barges were large but with a low bow they could only trade as far as Avonmouth, it was too dangerous to go on down to Swansea, especially in the winter with the rough seas experienced farther down the Bristol Channel.

Shortly after the skipper and mate arrived on board, the crew of both the *Wyesdale H* and *Wastdale H* let go their mooring ropes in darkness at Monk Meadow Dock to begin the three hour trip down the sixteen mile Gloucester & Sharpness Ship Canal to Sharpness. A short wait here before being called into the sea lock along with numerous other craft, some bound for Swansea, others for Avonmouth, vessels of all types, tugs with lighters, motor barges and many tanker barges plus a Dutch coaster bound back to the continent.

It was still early morning as all the craft locked out of Sharpness and made their way down the estuary, the sun having risen quite high bringing a magical look to the Severn. In the autumn sunshine the estuary

The WYESDALE H (inside) and the WASTDALE H together at Monk Meadow, Gloucester before departing on their fateful trip on 25th October 1960.

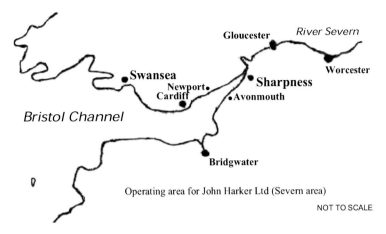

Gloucester

River Severn

Worcester

Swansea

Newport

Cardiff

Sharpness

Avonmouth

Bristol Channel

Bridgwater

Operating area for John Harker Ltd (Severn area)

NOT TO SCALE

looks at her best. The colours of the trees seen in the distance on the slopes of hills make the river sparkle like jewels on a crown. Streaks of light dazzle on the moving water as the tide recedes which help the barges on their way to Avonmouth.

Meanwhile at Swansea, craft bound for Sharpness would now be commencing their slow journey up the Bristol Channel. Amongst them the *Southdale H* and *Arkendale H*, tanker barges also owned by John Harker Limited. The *Arkendale H* was carrying a cargo of 296 tonnes of Britoleum (black oil), heavy oil that has to have heating coils running through the tanks to keep the oil in liquid form. This tanker barge was bound for Worcester and carried a crew of four men, no deckhand though, an extra engineer instead due to the fact that the barge was fitted with a boiler for the heating coils, which required two men in the engine-room. Another tanker barge leaving Swansea on that morning tide was the *Shell*

The ARKENDALE H arriving at Swansea and waiting to lock into the docks before loading at Queen's Dock.

Traveller bound for Gloucester with a cargo of 400 tonnes of petrol, crewed by five John Harker men (skipper, mate, engineer and two deckhands). It would have been a pleasant day coming up the Bristol Channel with clear blue skies, a warm sun and no wind. A lot different to days in winter when a strong gale is blowing, tossing these barges around like corks in a bath.

On arrival at Avonmouth various types of craft (cargo barges, tugs with lighters and the many tanker barges) would lock up into this vast port. Then the docks would be full of large freighters from all parts of the world, with cranes continually dipping and rising transferring cargo from ship to shore. The *Wastdale H* and *Wyesdale H* turned to port (left), heading out of the lock towards the far end of the oil dock, past the large mechanised oil boom, where they would be loaded. Three hours later all loaded it was now time to catch up on some sleep whilst waiting for the evening tide to take them back to Sharpness.

First lock out of Avonmouth was about 7.15pm so shortly before this time loaded craft would be milling around the lock entrance jostling for a good position to be first away. Although it was now dark, there was an eerie feel about the docks that night. The air was still, with little noise and experienced river men were commenting on how uneasy they felt about the trip upriver. A crewman from a barge that wasn't sailing that night had been offered a trip back to Sharpness so that he could spend some time with his family. He declined as he had a gut feeling that all was not well and there could be trouble ahead. Wise man!

As always many small craft were in that first lock out of Avonmouth and as the numerous types of vessels sped out into the mouth of the Severn Estuary, they could see slightly ahead of them lights from

The ARKENDALE H making her way down the Severn empty after discharging a cargo of heavy black oil at Worcester.
Following an overnight stop at Gloucester, vessel and crew will embark on the sea passage to Swansea to load another cargo of black oil.

The ARKENDALE H outside of Swansea Docks waiting to be called into the locks. Having loaded her cargo at the Queen's Dock they would go to anchor in Swansea Bay and wait for the flood tide to assist them back up the Bristol Channel, or in George's case, tie on the piers!

the tanker barges, which had come up from Swansea on the afternoon tide. Thirteen vessels proceeded up the estuary that evening, including the tug *Robert A* with three lighters laden with logs bound for Lydney. Visibility was about 2 to 3 miles so the crews went down into their warm cabins, leaving the masters of each barge alone in the wheelhouse to steer the barges on their course to Sharpness.

Although visibility had not been perfect coming up the estuary towards Sharpness, it had remained fairly clear until they arrived at the swinging light close to Berkeley Power Station, then they were surrounded by dense fog. This area has always been known for its thick fogs, caused by the low lying land on the foreshore being warmed by the autumn sunshine, then cooled by the evening air blowing over the land.

At about 9.30pm the bell in the accommodation of the *Wyesdale H* began to ring summoning the deckhand on deck to see what the skipper wanted. The lad was shocked to see that they were surrounded by a thick fog, so bad that it was impossible to see the bow from inside the wheelhouse. Orders were given to summon the mate and to get on the bow and listen for the foghorn at Sharpness. For the lad it was his first time out on the river in fog and having listened to the tales of those river men only a few hours previous, he wouldn't be sorry to see the safety of Sharpness Docks. Suddenly out of the fog appeared the bow of the *Wastdale H* with mate and lad also listening for the foghorn. The two lads on each barge exchanged words and then were lost again in the fog.

The tide was flowing up the river at about 5 knots that night and increasing in speed above Sharpness, giving each skipper the added problem of holding their barges safely in a position ready to make the difficult manoeuvre between the piers and into the lock. As the tide could be more powerful than the engines on the barges, it required the skippers to turn their barges around to stem the tide whilst passing Berkeley Power Station, then carefully dropping back slowly towards Sharpness whilst still punching the tide, barely holding themselves against the strong flowing current.

The *Arkendale H* was 40.3 metres in length and 6.7 metres wide and had been built as a dumb tanker barge in 1937 and converted to a motor tanker barge in 1948. Skippered by George Thompson (35), who had swung his barge around earlier at Berkeley Power Station to stem the tide and as he did so he noticed the fog coming across the river from the foreshore. Before being completely enveloped in the fog he had managed to reach Sharpness Piers and as well as sounding his horn, kept a listen out for the fog siren, located on the end of one of the piers. Pushing ahead against the tide George Thompson could again hear the fog siren on his port bow but as he began to make the turn to go between the piers, he saw the tug *Addie* with a string of barges in tow going across his bows. To avoid a collision he took power off the engine of the *Arkendale H*, which unfortunately caused the barge to drift past the piers again. Finding himself in comparatively slack water above the old harbour entrance he began to line his vessel up to proceed back down the river to the harbour entrance.

Joey Lane, skipper of the tug *Addie*, had picked up the sound of the Sharpness fog siren and using that as his bearing speedily got the tug and tow between the piers and into the lock. He hadn't realised though, that his tug and the *Arkendale H* had been on a converging course, the fog so thick that he could only find his way between the piers by taking a sound bearing from the fog siren.

Shortly after the *Arkendale H* had passed Sharpness Piers, the tanker barge *Shell Traveller* entered the harbour whereupon the assistant harbour master shouted to Tommy Carter, (master of the tanker barge), informing him that there was a vessel some way up the river. Tommy Carter realised that it could be the *Arkendale H* and tried to make contact by the radiotelephone but received no reply. He then called the *Southdale H* and asked her master to call the *Arkendale H* but he also failed to get a reply.

With full power on his 8 cylinder Gleniffer engine George Thompson lined up the *Arkendale H* to begin the crawl against the tide back to the harbour entrance. At best, his vessel would only manage 7 knots and that was with the propeller in peak condition. (Upstream of Gloucester the Severn took its toll on barges continually rubbing the bed of the river, damaging the propellers whilst striking submerged debris). As he turned his wheel to alter course Thompson's mate, Percy Simmonds (34), shouted out that there was another vessel fine on their port bow. It was the W*astdale H* with master James Dew (42), who was a relief skipper on the barge and only on his second trip.

The *Wastdale H* had been built at Sharpness nine years earlier in 1951 with a length of 39.9 metres and 6.4 metres wide and with a good propeller could obtain a maximum of 7 knots when loaded. Unknown to James Dew he had followed the same course as the *Arkendale H* and got himself too close to the bank below Sharpness Piers. Unfortunately the stern of the *Wastdale H* touched the bank and held on the mud and had to take assistance from another vessel to be pulled off. Dew too, passed the harbour entrance losing the sound of the foghorn with his vessel being taken with the current towards the old and disused dock entrance. George Thompson was still sounding his whistle and James Dew on hearing this could then pick out the mast lights of the *Arkendale H*. The mate of the *Arkendale H* shouted that there was another vessel on their port bow.

Thompson recognised her as the *Wastdale H* and knew that Dew was still a stranger to her. He shouted to him, "Do you know where you are?". Without waiting for a reply he told Dew that they were abreast of the Old Dock entrance. Slowly both vessels came together and a worry to both skippers back aft in their wheelhouses, was that the suction created would make it difficult to break apart.

James Dew gave his 4 cylinder Ruston 7 engine full power and the wheel hard to starboard [right] to try to push the *Arkendale H* away, whilst George Thompson gave his vessel port (left) wheel to keep the barge heading into the tide. With both men having great difficulty in breaking the two barges apart, they could not hold the vessels against the tide and soon the vessels became out of control as they were taken out into the fast flowing current. The barges still locked together travelled sideways up the river heading towards the Severn Railway Bridge.

All eight crew of both vessels were on deck, the two skippers in the wheelhouses, some on the bow and the remainder stood at the stern. They had four minutes of fear as both barges fought to break apart, George Thompson put his wheel hard to starboard with an endeavour to swing the barge around and stem the tide again. Meanwhile James Dew put his engines full astern to hopefully pull away from the *Arkendale H*. Too late, for suddenly the Severn Railway Bridge was looming up on his port side and the barge struck column number 17 with the bluff of the port bow. The bridge shook with the impact as the barges lay against the column, then the *Wastdale H* turned over onto her port side with the force of the tide pushing the *Arkendale H* on top of the sinking barge. George Thompson was coming out of the wheelhouse as two spans of the bridge dropped from 21 metres onto the two barges, the impact throwing him against the bulkhead and he was temporarily knocked unconscious. James Dew was thrown into the water from his barge with the impact but managed to cling to a rail and climb back on board.

Meanwhile at 10.16pm signalman Donald Dobbs had given the all clear for the Lydney to Stoke train to cross the Severn Railway Bridge. After the train had passed over the bridge another railway worker, Mr T. C. Francis, had left the Severn Bridge station signal box at 10.30pm to walk down to the bridge and could see the lights of Sharpness and hear the roar of the tide as it swept up through the columns of the bridge. Suddenly he saw a sheet of red flame shoot up into the sky from beneath the bridge, followed by an explosion, then silence. He ran onto the bridge and was horrified to see the two tankers burning below with flames almost reaching the decking of the bridge. Without hesitation he ran back to the signal box to telephone the emergency services. On returning to the bridge he could see the gaping hole where the two spans had been, with the gas main and electric cable ripped away. The barges were still burning fiercely and by this time the tide had carried both craft together with two spans of the bridge across them farther upstream of the bridge where they grounded on a sandbank.

George Thompson quickly regained consciousness and made his way aft to the stern of the *Arkendale H,* where he could see two of his crewmen standing in the well deck. He knew that both men could not swim so gave them each a life ring and stood between them and told them to jump into the river with him. The river was ablaze with petrol from the ruptured cargo tanks of the W*astdale H* and the *Arkendale H* was on fire as well and sinking. Thompson jumped and as he hit the water, he looked back only to see that both crewmen had stayed behind. He had no choice but to swim clear of the wreckage away from the burning fuel oil.

James Dew, clinging to the rail managed to pull himself up and clamber onto the *Arkendale H* where he realised that her engines were still running ahead, turning the propeller which by now was out of the water. He tried to make his way to the wheelhouse to stop the propeller but as he got there it burst into flames. As he made his way to the stern end, he could see the remaining two crewmen had inflated a life raft but it drifted away as it was thrown into the water. Dew told the men that they must get off the barge and led them down the deck where they were able to walk into the water.

Engineer, Jack Cooper (43), was swept by the current around to the stern of the barge where he sustained injuries to his back from the revolving propeller of the *Arkendale H.* Jack, although in pain, couldn't face the prospect of being burnt to death by the sea of fire from the petrol around him. He decided it would be best to give up the struggle of staying afloat and to sink beneath the burning oil. As he was sinking, he began to have thoughts of his family at home and realised how much they would miss him, so he fought his way back to the surface. The tide, now ebbing, had taken him to Wellhouse Bay, (a little way below the bridge on the Lydney side), to leave him stranded on a sandbank but still alive.

The sound of the explosion could be heard by crew members of the *Wyesdale H,* which was still punching against the incoming tide trying to locate Sharpness piers in the thick fog. They could see an orange glow in the distance, in the direction of the Severn Railway Bridge and their first thoughts were that workmen had had an accident with machinery or gas cylinders on the bridge. The cargo of petrol, which had escaped from the ruptured cargo tanks of the *Wastdale H,* had ignited both vessels and the Severn as well, fortunately with the current taking it upstream away from the numerous other craft still waiting entry to Sharpness further downstream from the railway bridge. The heat from the severe fire was so intense that it cleared the fog thus assisting the remaining vessels still out in the river to make a safe entry into the lock at Sharpness. Although bound for Lydney, Robert Young of Bristol, skipper of the tug *Robert A*, decided to make the safer entry into Sharpness, with the river ablaze and the tide still flowing he thought it too dangerous to go back across the river. Tommy Carter, master of the *Shell Traveller*, who had been patiently waiting in the lock to be levelled up for entry into Sharpness Docks, asked the lock foreman to fill the lock quickly so that he could get his vessel tied up in the docks and then possibly assist with rescuing crew members of the two stricken vessels.

At the time of the accident the Chief Fire Officer of Gloucestershire Fire Service together with one of his Divisional Officers and a Home Office Inspector had been travelling from Lydney on the A48 road towards Gloucester, when they saw the glow from the explosion in the direction of the River Severn. Chief Officer Payne radioed his control at Cheltenham and was told that no call had been received regarding the explosion and on hearing this they decided to drive down to the Severn Bridge Station. They were horrified to see that the river was ablaze as far as the eye could see for at least a mile upstream of the bridge and all across the river, which is three quarters of a mile wide at this point. Fire Service control was informed of what he saw and they confirmed that other calls were now coming in from members of the public. Berkeley Police confirmed that they had received a call stating that a petrol tanker barge was ablaze on the Sharpness Canal. With the confusing locations being given to the emergency services regarding the fire, the Fire Service dispatched fire engines from both sides of the river. The Chief Fire Officer had the agonising 40 mile drive via Gloucester to reach Sharpness before he could take charge of operations.

On jumping from the stern of the *Arkendale H* George Thompson found himself in thick, black oil. The river was on fire spreading out behind him as he swam away from the barges, swimming as close as he dare to the fire he could see the *Arkendale H* was going down by the bow, exposing the still revolving propeller. The *Wastdale H* was one mass of flames with both barges straddled by the two spans and railway lines of the bridge, still afloat and drifting slowly with the tide. George swam with the current, which was taking him upstream towards Gloucester, still fully clothed accept for his shoes, covered in the thick, heavy crude oil from the cargo his barge had been carrying. He was hollering all the time and once heard someone else shouting for help, "Is that you Bob", he cried but got no response.

The current had taken George three miles upstream before he was able to reach the banks of the Severn on the Lydney side. Still hollering he

The scene at daybreak the following day.

Two spans missing from the Severn Railway Bridge.

Captain George Thompson, skipper of the ARKENDALE H, at home in bed in his home at Gloucester talking to fellow Harker colleague Davy Jones.

Davy Jones had recently lost one of his legs in a accident on another John Harker ship, the SOUTHDALE H.

Photo from E. Parker collection

The Severn Railway Bridge shortly after the accident with Sharpness in the background pulled himself out of the water but soon became very cold so dropped himself back into the river and lay submerged under the water to help keep warm. A farmer had heard all the commotion from the explosion together with the shouts for help and went down to the river bank to investigate whereby he came across George Thompson huddled in the water still hollering. The farmer took George back to his farmhouse at Poulton Court, where his wife insisted he come inside and sit by the warm fire, although he was covered in dirty, black oil. An ambulance arrived at the house to take George to hospital and the driver told him that another survivor had been picked up further downstream near to Lydney.

James Dew, like George Thompson, swam away from the wrecked tanker barges and after a long time in the river reached shore on the Lydney side above the bridge. Basil Freeman, who lived near the bridge, had gone down to the shore and heard shouting from someone in the water. He shone his torch, shouted encouragement but realised the man was being carried away from him by the current. He scrambled across mud and rocks for half a mile before he was able to pull the man out of the cold water. Wearing his life jacket and also covered in black oil James Dew was taken to a local inn to await the ambulance, the same one that was carrying the other survivor, George Thompson. Both men were then taken to Lydney Hospital.

From Lydney to Blakeney the word soon spread that there had been an accident on the River Severn above Sharpness and it wasn't long before crowds thronged the banks, horrified at the sight of flames relentlessly spreading over the river. Police Sergeant Roy Cottle of Blakeney said, "The cries of help heard that night reminded him of the terrible cries heard when on convoy duty during the Second World War after a ship had gone down". Police and others carried out an exhaustive search of the river on the Lydney side until 3 am when they realised the tide would have carried any survivors away from them. The police also organised search parties with boats from villages above Lydney.

Tommy Carter having safely tied up his vessel the *Shell Traveller* in Sharpness Docks, together with his crew, ran to the end of the piers where they could hear shouting coming from upstream of the dock entrance. He saw a small rowing boat lying on the shore and with the help of others had it loaded onto a lorry and taken to Purton, a village situated at the end of the Gloucester & Sharpness Canal. With local inhabitants and firemen the boat was taken from the lorry and carried across the marshy land to the waters edge. Assisting Tommy Carter was Charles Henderson, a carpenter from Berkeley Power Station, who accompanied him out onto the river to look for survivors. These were brave men, who at great risk to themselves, rowed the boat close to the flames and at one stage had to zig-zag across to the Lydney side to escape from the fire. They could hear shouts for help, sometimes quite close, other times appearing to drift farther away. After some time they found Jack Cooper, engineer from the *Arkendale H*, who was exhausted and still wearing his life ring, as well as suffering great pain from the gash in his back. He was landed on the Lydney side of the Severn and taken to the local hospital.

The Fire Service was faced with numerous problems. The first being that although they could see the burning vessels, it was proving impossible to get to them. Appliances had been deployed both sides of the Severn and with the aid of their radios they were able to be kept informed of any plan of action. On the advice of the Sharpness Harbour Master it was decided that no appliance or fire fighters would be sent out to the fire that night as it was considered, due to the hazardous nature of the tides, to be too dangerous to risk mens' lives. A fireboat was stationed at Sharpness, but was only suitable to be used in the dock or on the canal, it was quite unsuitable for use on the river, especially in the conditions that night. Fire hose was laid out at both Sharpness Docks and Lydney Harbour in case the fire should spread from the river to property on the shore at either location.

People on both sides of the river were, by now, wandering down to the foreshore to witness the terrible tragedy. Many thought the gas pipeline across the bridge had fractured and caught fire. In fact due to the prompt action of an employee at the Sharpness gasholder the supply had been shut off before the escaping gas could ignite. Various impressions of what happened that night began to emerge later, many at the time not really knowing what was going on out in the river. A young lady working on the Merchant Navy Training Ship *Vindicatrix* at Sharpness has a lasting memory of the strong smell of petrol fumes wafting over the estuary.

At 5am next morning vessels began leaving Sharpness Docks for the three hour trip up the Gloucester & Sharpness Canal to Gloucester. As they passed beneath the Severn Railway Bridge on the canal between Sharpness and Purton, they could see the two tanker barges out in the river still smouldering, reminding all crews of the terrible accident the night before.

Only three men survived the accident, the two skippers and an engineer. Five men were deemed to have been killed in the explosion, from the *Arkendale H* mate Percy Simmonds (34) and 2nd engineer Robert Nibblett (25). From the *Wastdale H* mate Jack Dudfield (46), engineer Alex Bullock (40) and deckhand Malcolm Hart (17) were missing. It is known that Percy Simmonds was unable to swim and that he had entered the water with Jack Cooper. Percy's body was recovered from the river on the Lydney side next day. The other four missing crewmen were last seen on the bow of their vessels before being taken by the tide into the railway bridge, killed by the collision and explosion.

That same morning at 7.30am the Fire Service and Police accompanied by Sharpness Harbour Master, walked out to the stranded barges. About half a mile from shore the *Arkendale H* lay on an even keel whilst the *Wastdale H* lay on her starboard side. Due to the incoming tide and the difficulty of walking on the mud, sandbanks and quicksand it was decided to abandon any search until the next day.

During the next morning it proved to be difficult to search the vessels owing to the amount of oil and water in the barges. Arrangements were made that day for the transportation of light pumps out to the wrecks to enable the oil and water to be pumped out.

At 7am on Friday 28th October all the pumps had been assembled on the shore at Purton ready to be taken out to the wrecked vessels. Due to the strong tides of the last couple of days the *Wastdale H* had regained an even keel and was surrounded by water to a depth of 2 metres. The job of getting the pumps out to the barges proved to be far more difficult than anticipated. The pumps had been placed on makeshift wooden sledges and pulled across the mud but halfway across they began to sink into the sand almost disappearing into the quicksand. Arriving at the vessels it was only possible to get on board by clambering up the railway lines that still lay across the barges. The search was hampered by the presence of oil, water and now fumes in both tanker barges and the operation was once again abandoned until the next day.

The Chief Fire Officer sought the co-operation of the Royal Air Force to airlift a special pump from Purton onto the deck of the *Wastdale H* but that day dawned with news that the helicopter had developed engine trouble and was not available. Orders were given to manhandle the pump across the sands to the barge, where it was used to pump out all the oil and water and a full search with firemen in breathing apparatus revealed nothing. A similar operation on the *Arkendale H* proved impossible due to her being holed below the waterline. So men with probes prodded into the engine room as best they could for bodies. At 11am that day all men and equipment were removed from the vessels due to the incoming tide.

On Sunday 30th October between 7am and 11.30am the army placed explosive charges at the bow and stern of both vessels to sink them into the mud of the estuary to prevent their movement in the river. At low water they can still be seen today from both banks of the river.

The bodies of the missing men were eventually all recovered from various locations along the Severn Estuary.

© Chris Witts

(Above) After 50 years of tide sweeping against the wrecks, the name ARKENDALE H is still visible on the bow! (Below) The stern end of the ARKENDALE H showing the pump house and above it where the wooden wheelhouse was.

© Chris Witts

© Chris Witts

Above) Damage to the stern of the WASTDALE H where the army had placed explosive charges.   (Below) The bow of the WASTDALE H is not visible above the waterline due no doubt to the damage caused by the explosive charges.

© Chris Witts

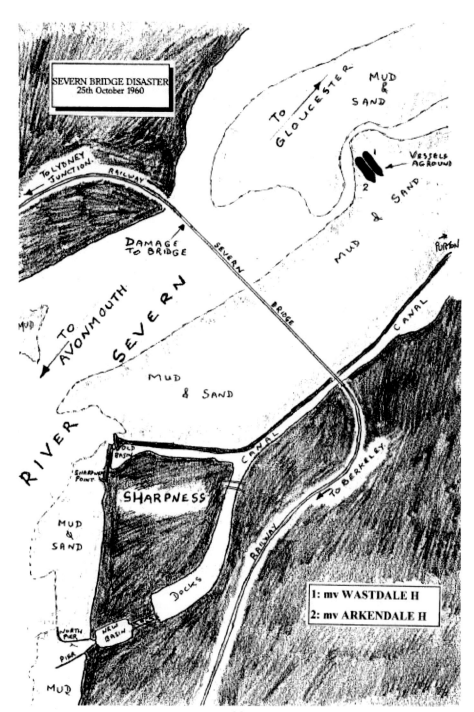

SEVERN BRIDGE DISASTER
25th October 1960

TO LYDNEY JUNCTION.

RAILWAY

TO GLOUCESTER

MUD & SAND

VESSELS AGROUND

1

2

MUD & SAND

DAMAGE TO BRIDGE

SEVERN BRIDGE

PURTON

TO AVONMOUTH

MUD

SEVERN

MUD & SAND

CANAL

RIVER

CANAL

TO BERKELEY

MUD & SAND

OLD BASIN

SHARPNESS POINT

SHARPNESS

RAILWAY

MUD & SAND

DOCKS

1: mv WASTDALE H
2: mv ARKENDALE H

NORTH PIER

NEW BASIN

PIER

MUD

GLOUCESTERSHIRE FIRE SERVICE
RESEARCH REPORT
SEVERN BRIDGE SHARPNESS

1   DATE AND TIME OF CALL AND ADDRESS OF PREMISES
    Tuesday 25th October 1960 at 2235 hours
    the m.v. WASTDALE H and ARKENDALE H on River Severn
    between Sharpness and Purton.

2   TRADE OR BUSINESS CARRIED
    Ship Owners: Transportation of petroleum by sea, river and canal.

3   WHERE AND AT WHAT TIME THE FIRE ACTUALLY ORIGINATED
    In m.v. WASTDALE H at about 2230 hours.

4   NUMBER OF PUMPS USED TO EXTINGUISH FIRE
    Four water tenders, one foam tender and one water tender specially
    designed for generating foam in bulk were dispatched to the scene of the
    fire; five to Sharpness Docks and one to Lydney Docks on the opposite side of
    the river. Due to its location the fire was inaccessible and no pumps were
    used. Lines of hose were, however, laid out on both piers at Sharpness Dock
    entrance and on Lydney Docks to be ready in the event of any burning oil
    being washed into the vicinity by the currents

5   PARTICULARS OF CONSTRUCTION
    Steel construction, diesel motor vessel WASTDALE H
    Gross tonnage 229.33, Net tonnage 132.49
    Steel construction, diesel motor vessel ARKENDALE H
    Gross tonnage 229.18, Net tonnage 112.03

6   SUPPOSED CAUSE OF FIRE
    Electrical or mechanical spark ignited leaking petroleum spirit.

7   GENERAL DESCRIPTION OF DAMAGE
    m.v. WASTDALE H and m.v. ARKENDALE H severely damaged by impact
    and fire and the whole of the contents of both vessels consisting of 351 tons
    of Premium petroleum spirit and 296 tons of petroleum fuel oil respectively
    destroyed by fire.

    One pier and two spans [each span about 170'] of single track .75 mile long
    railway bridge destroyed by impact and collapse. A 12 inch diameter gas main
    situated alongside the railway track and supplying the Forest of Dean area
    was broken away for the distance of the bridge damage.

8   BUILDINGS EXPOSED TO RISK OF FIRE AND WHETHER THESE WERE
     AFFECTED IN ANY WAY
     A mixture of petroleum spirit and fuel oil spread over a considerable area of
     the river, which was about .75 of a mile wide at the scene of the incident.
     Precautionary measures were taken on both banks of the river, but due to
     sand and mud banks on each side of the main stream the fire did not threaten
     any buildings.

9   SERIOUS CASUALTIES
     Each vessel was carrying a crew of four men. Out of the total of eight men
     involved, two reached the river bank, aided by their life jackets, one was
     rescued by boatmen from the Tites Point, Purton, four were later taken dead
     from the river and one is still missing, presumed dead.

10   NOTES OF UNUSUAL FEATURES
     During the evening of Tuesday 25th October 1960 some sixteen ships were on
     the River Severn travelling from Avonmouth to Sharpness on the incoming
     tide.
     In the area of Sharpness a dense fog came down reducing visibility in places
     to a few yards. Fog sirens were in operation at Sharpness Docks and
     Sharpness Point.
     The normal procedure for vessels entering the docks on the incoming tide is
     to pass the entrance, circle and come in against the tide by the North Pier.
     It is understood that eight vessels entered the docks at about 2250 hours and
     three at about 2340 hours. WASTDALE H and ARKENDALE H, owned by
     John Harker Ltd., of Knottingley, Yorks, did not enter the dock.
     WASTDALE H, a tanker of 229 grt, carrying 351 tons of Premium petroleum
     spirit, was skippered by James Dew [42] of 15 Hudson Street, Burnham-on
     Sea, with a crew of three men:
     Hubert Jack Dudfield [46] of Widdale, Gloucester Road, Staunton, Glos., Alex
     Albert Bullock [40] of 154 Melbourne St., Gloucester and Malcolm Hart [17] of
     115 High Street, Gloucester.
     ARKENDALE H, a tanker of 229 grt, carrying 296 tons of fuel oil, was
     skippered by George Horace Thompson [33] of Flat 1, 18 Bisley Road,
     Tuffley, Gloucester, with a crew of three men:
     Percy Alexander Simmonds [34] of 27 Kitchener Avenue, Gloucester, George
     William Cooper [43] of 5 Cornish Houses, Buckshafts Road, Cinderford, Glos.
     and Robert John Niblett [25] of West View, Canal Bank, Hardwicke.
     It appears that due to the thick fog both vessels missed the entrance to the
     docks and were swept up river by the incoming tide, which is understood, was
     running at about 8 knots.
     During their endeavour to locate the dock entrance they either collided or ran

28

alongside each other and were unable to break apart before being swept against one of the piers of the .75 mile long, single track railway bridge carrying the line between Lydney and Sharpness.

The force of the impact carried away the pier which allowed two spans to fall. The railway lines fell across both vessels holding them together.

Both vessels were severely damaged, allowing the contents of the tanks to leak away. It is believed that vapour from the tanker carrying petroleum spirit was ignited, either by a mechanical spark due to stone and concrete striking the steel of the vessel, or by an electrical spark when the electric wiring operating at 110 volts D.C. was severed.

It is understood that flames from the burning vessels were higher than the bridge, which is some 70' above high water and a mixture of burning petroleum spirit and fuel oil floated for one mile upstream until, the tide turned, it spread over almost the whole of the .75 mile width of the river.

The two vessels, blazing furiously and still held together by the railway lines, floated about half a mile towards Gloucester, where they went aground on a sandbank.

The river above Sharpness is not navigable due to the very treacherous currents and sandbanks.

The fire was observed by people on the river bank and the Fire Service was called by exchange telephone at 2235 hours.

It would appear that members of the crews were on deck keeping a lookout and that when the bridge was struck they were either thrown or jumped into the water. Cries for help were clearly heard by people on the banks of the river, including at Purton about a mile upstream.

At this time the Chief Officer and a Divisional Officer, who, with the Home Office Inspector, had been visiting stations, were travelling from Lydney to Cheltenham when a glow suddenly appeared in the sky in the direction of the River Severn.

It was ascertained by radio to Fire Control that no call had been received to any fire in the area.

As the glow persisted a visit was paid to Severn Bridge Station at the side of the river when upon arrival, it was found that the surface of the river was alight as far as could be seen. The fire was causing the fog to disperse and the estimated distance of vision was about half a mile.

This information was passed to Fire Control by radio. Simultaneously with the receipt of this message a call was received by exchange telephone from Berkeley Police stating that a petrol tanker was on fire on the Sharpness Canal.

Although the Home Office Inspector and Chief Fire Officer were within half a mile of the fire they had to travel 40 miles via Gloucester bridge to proceed to the scene of the incident. In the meantime four appliances were dispatched to the area of the fire.

It was quickly ascertained that the burning vessel, (it was not then known whether one or two vessels were involved), was on the river and not on the canal.

This was an extremely frustrating job as the glow could be seen through the fog but it was impossible to get near the fire. There were three problems which could not be resolved: [a] Where the vessel or vessels actually were: [b] If they were ascertained, could they be reached? And [c] If this were possible could a rescue of any personnel be carried out?

The radio was a great asset for this particular operation and was in use continuously in organising the disposition of the appliances along the river banks.

On the advice of the Harbour Master it was decided that it was quite useless for appliances to be taken out to the fire; it should be appreciated that the River Severn is particularly treacherous above the entrance to Sharpness Docks due to the strong and unknown currents, sand and mud banks.

The fire boat stationed at Sharpness docks is only suitable for use either in the dock or in the canal and was totally unsuitable for use on the river, particularly under the conditions at the time out on the Severn.

Advice was then sought from the Harbour Master as to the direction of the current on the turning of the tide and with this point in mind, three lines of hose were laid out in the Sharpness Docks area and one at Lydney Docks on the opposite side of the river so as to be ready in the event of any burning oil being brought into the vicinity of the currents.

Bristol City Fire Brigade were warned of the possible hazard of fuel going down the river. They were also asked if their fire boat could be brought up to the scene of the incident but it was understood that this could not be done.

The Fire Service personnel loaded a row boat onto a lorry at Sharpness for transportation to Purton, a small hamlet about two miles upstream, where they assisted in manhandling it across the foreshore and launching it with the skipper of one of the tankers which had docked and one other man. They were successful in rescuing one member of the crew who was landed on the opposite bank of the river.

When the vessels damaged the bridge they also severed a 12 inch diameter gas main, the leaking gas from which did not become ignited. Immediate action was taken to shut off the supply.

During the night J W Dew, G H Thompson, [the two skippers], and G W Cooper, whose rescue is referred to above, were recovered from the river alive and the following day, A Simmonds [dead]; all from the Forest of Dean side of the river.

At 0730 hours on the 26th October it is understood that the Sharpness Harbour Master and Police went out to the stranded vessels. At the time the ARKENDALE H was on an even keel and the WASTDALE H lying on its starboard side. Owing to the incoming tide and the fact that the vessels were lying about half a mile from the river bank, with the intervening space consisting of mud flats, sandbanks and quicksand, no further approach could be made until the following day at low water. A further search was made the following morning, but due to the quantity of water and oil in the vessels only a small section could be searched.

During the day arrangements were made to transport a light portable pump to the wrecks to pump out the water and the remaining oil to enable a search to be made of the interiors of the vessels for the missing members of the crews. At 0700 hours on the morning of the 28th October the pump and ancillary equipment were assembled on the river bank and the task of transporting them across the flats commenced. At that time due to the tides, the WASTDALE H had regained an even keel and both vessels were surrounded by water to a depth of about seven feet. By climbing along the railway lines which straddled the vessels it was possible to climb aboard. The pump was carried across the mud flats, then, mounted on an improved sledge, was dragged across the mud. About halfway across the personnel and pump began to sink into the sand and it was only with extreme difficulty, after the pump had almost disappeared in the quicksand that it was extricated and with the help of a ladder as a lever, moved to firmer ground. A search was made within the vessels as far as possible but, due to the presence of oil, water and fumes, much of the interior was inaccessible.

At this point the operation was abandoned until low water the following morning.

During the day the Chief Officer made arrangements for a new type of ultra light pump to be obtained from Coventry and, with the co-operation of the Royal Air Force, for a helicopter to carry it from a selected spot at Sharpness directly to the deck of the WASTDALE H.

Accordingly, personnel and equipment with the Chief Fire Officer in charge assembled at Sharpness at 0700 hours on Saturday the 29th October. Soon after arrival, a message was received by radio to the effect that the helicopter had engine trouble and would not be available. All personnel and equipment were taken to Purton and the equipment was manhandled across the soft sand to the vessels. The pump was taken on board and the cabin of the WASTDALE H drained and searched by personnel wearing breathing apparatus, without result.

A similar attempt was made to pump water from the engine room of the ARKENDALE H but the vessel was apparently holed below the water line and no progress was made. The engine room was, however, probed as far as possible without any sign of a body.

Shortly before 1100 hours the men were withdrawn and, with all gear moved off to the shore in the face of the incoming tide. It was decided that the possibility of any bodies remaining in the wrecks was very remote.

On Sunday, 30th October between 0700 hours and 1130 hours, the army placed explosive charges to the stern and bow of the wrecks to prevent any danger of their moving with the coming of high tides.

Chief Fire Officer Payne (centre) in charge of the fire service personnel who had the difficult job of searching for bodies within the two wrecks.

Looking towards the stern of both vessels.

Fire Service photographs taken the following day

Firemen pumping out water from the inside of one of the vessels.
Firemen working on the stern of the WASTDALE H

The Official Inquiry

An official inquiry into the accident between the two vessels and the Severn Railway Bridge was conducted at Bristol in May 1961 before Waldo Porges Q.C. During the three day hearing Maurice Edwards, Senior Nautical Surveyor from the Ministry of Transport, showed concern for the safety of the River Severn and was perturbed at these casualties especially with the loss of the *BP Explorer* in the Severn Estuary with five men (16th February 1961).

During his statement Capt. James Dew said, "*I found I was going under the bridge and the stern went comfortably under but she hit the pillar with the port bow. When I found that the stern had got through I eased up. I thought she might canter through. I pulled astern to see if I could canter off the pillar. I was doing that when we actually hit. I don't think we actually completed it. I was flung down down into the doorway of the wheelhouse and found myself in the water. She was on her beam-end. I went over the side and grabbed a guard rail and got myself back on deck. There was a terrific list on her and she was all on fire........*".

Waldo Porges Q.C. in his summing up said, "The disaster occurred without any fault in navigation for which either master can be blamed". The Court then recommended that all concerned in the administration of the harbour and approaches should consider it a matter of joint responsibility to examine the whole situation in detail with a view to improving existing conditions.

© *Chris Witts*

The Severn Railway Bridge – History and Demolition

The Building of the Bridge

On 18th July 1872 the Severn Bridge Railway Company was formed to provide a link for the Great Western and the Severn & Wye Railway at Lydney to the Midland Railway at Sharpness. This would be of benefit to the Midland Railway as construction of the new dock at Sharpness had begun the previous year and the railway company saw the potential of bringing coal in from the Forest of Dean.

Following three years of planning, construction finally began in 1875 to a design of Mr T E Harrison with the contract for building the bridge awarded to Hamiltons Windsor Iron Works Company Limited of London. A small gathering of local people had met on the foreshore at Purton [Lydney side] to witness on Thursday 3rd July 1875 the laying of the foundation stone at precisely 2pm, by Mr W C Lucy, chairman of the Severn Bridge Railway Company, who then made the obligatory speech expected at these occasions and laid a two ton block on solid rock.

Then followed four years of construction, sometimes not all going to plan, certain work falling behind schedule but having overcome the might of the powerful tides of the Severn, the bridge was finally built. From the Lydney shore twelve masonry arches crossed the mud flats, then the three-quarter mile wide river was bridged by twenty-one spans, with a swing bridge crossing the Gloucester & Sharpness Ship Canal. Sadly, as was the case then with constructing something as large as this, fatalities occurred.

The first happened on the 8th January 1878 when workman John Tomkins of Ruardean was killed, not on the bridge but at the nearby tunnel workings at Purton, [Lydney side]. A section of timber weighing one ton fell on him when the securing rope slipped. A foreman employed by the tunnel construction company was severely reprimanded by the coroner for his lack of attention to safety and supervision.

A year later on Wednesday 1st March, William Aston aged 64 of Lydney was killed in a fall on the viaduct at Purton [Lydney side]. The inquest at Lydney Police Station was told that William Aston and a young chap called Drew were operating a travelling crane carrying stone blocks along the viaduct. The crane travelled on rails and as it was in the centre of the viaduct a strong wind blew up for about ten minutes. The wind caught the crane making it travel too fast along the rails until it crashed into some timber staging falling seventy feet to the deck below. Aston was thrown twenty-five feet onto the staging and suffered serious injuries while his mate, Drew, escaped injury. William Aston was removed to the new Severn Bridge Station where he died at 1.40pm.

The third and final fatality occurred as the end of construction of the bridge was in sight. It happened on Saturday 3rd June 1879, as Thomas Roberts of Viney Hill fell from the bridge into the river while engaged in the erection of the last 312' span. As he fell, he struck the staging causing him severe injuries but he was only in the river for five minutes as an alert boatman had spotted him falling and was able to rescue him. He died shortly after being taken to the Engineer's Rooms at Purton Manor, [Lydney side].

The first train to test the bridge left Lydney Station at lunchtime on Wednesday 3rd September 1879 with directors and managers of the companies involved travelling in a luxurious carriage to Sharpness. On the return trip at 2.30pm the train stopped at the bridge to allow the passengers to alight and inspect the magnificent bridge.

The first collision with the bridge by a boat could be logged as happening on the 6th September 1879. Thomas Shaw from Gatcombe, proprietor of a fishing business, together with his brother William and friend Thomas Margrate had been at Avonmouth to purchase an anchor for one of their boats. Returning back to Gatcombe on a strong tide they made an effort to run through No 19 span of the Severn Railway Bridge but as they rowed through they were caught in a large eddy and turned broadside across the tide. The large boat was taken out of control into the timber staging around the column, which subsequently cut it in two. All three men clung onto the staging but that which Thomas Shaw was hanging onto, collapsed throwing him into the fast flowing tide which then swept him away.

With some difficulty William Shaw and Thomas Margrate climbed the staging up onto the deck of the bridge and walked along the track to Sharpness to the contractors office near the old docks. Here they borrowed a boat to row back to the other side of the river and on up to Gatcombe. The following day divers searched the staging below water level to search for the missing body but nothing was found. It was not until the 9th September that the body of Thomas Shaw was recovered from the river by David Long of Framilode.

The great day finally arrived, Friday 17th October 1879, the official opening of the Severn Railway Bridge. Crowds of people gathered at both Sharpness and Lydney with special trains bringing folk from Gloucester and elsewhere. A field at Sharpness had been turned into a fairground and on the other side of the river, the Lydney brass band turned out to add their bit to the occasion. The steam locomotive, 'Maid Marian' waiting at Lydney, was covered in bunting as were the sides of the bridge, even ships in the dock were dressed overall, with the grey clouds of the morning vanishing, giving way to clear skies and sun.

Between two and three hundred official guests gathered to see the chairman of the company, Mr W C Lucy, together with the Earl of Bathurst, Earl of Ducie, Mr F Allport, Mr G W Keeling and Mr W P Price climb aboard 'Maid Marian' at noon ready for the trip across the bridge. With whistle blowing the steam train slowly pulled away out onto the bridge to fire its own royal salute, as fog signals had been placed on the line, one each side of the twenty-one spans.

After a brief halt at Sharpness the train once again crossed the bridge but at the first 312' span, the train stopped to allow Lucy to alight and tighten the last bolt on the bridge. When he completed this minor task, he declared the bridge open for rail traffic.

Ironically the date of the opening of the bridge, October 17th 1879 was exactly one hundred years after the completion of that other great bridge on the Severn, Iron Bridge, the first bridge to be made of iron in England.

Demolition of the Bridge

A year after the disaster of 1960 there were mixed feelings about whether the bridge should be rebuilt or demolished. To rebuild the bridge would have cost £312,000 against an estimated cost of £250,00 to demolish it. Local feelings were to rebuild the bridge, as it had provided a vital link between the communities of Sharpness and Lydney. The Education Committee of Gloucestershire County Council was worried the affect would have on transporting the children to each side of the river. Until the accident schoolchildren from Sharpness had used the daily train to take them to and from Lydney Grammar School. Major E Mealing, chairman of the Highways Committee said that considering the small difference of £60,000 between restoration and demolition he thought the British Transport Commission should rebuild the bridge.

Whatever the outcome of BTC's decision whether to rebuild or demolish, the bridge had to be made safe, so in early December 1961 an underwater examination of the piers was carried out. Extensive damage to pier sixteen was found, it was leaning towards the Sharpness bank and in danger of collapsing into the river. A contract was awarded to Peter Lind & Co Ltd to erect a temporary trestle under the bridge close to the damaged pier, many people thought this to be the first stage of reconstruction of the bridge.

Days before the company began work on erecting the trestle another drama took place out in the river. On Friday 17th February 1961 an upturned tanker barge drifted out of control and struck pier twenty as it came down river on the ebbing tide. Then on the next tide this same hulk drifted back upriver with the incoming flow and floated through the bridge to finally rest on the mud at Awre. It was estimated that this incident had added another £12,740 worth of damage to the bridge.

Peter Lind & Co had hired, at a cost of £375 per week, a twin hulled floating crane from Liverpool, named *Tweedledum & Tweedledee*. More drama was to take place on the Severn, for on Friday 14th April 1961, this too broke away from its anchorage near the bridge and drifted upriver on the flood tide. Soon after the alarm was raised at Sharpness men boarded a small vessel, the *Magpie* and set off to Awre where the floating crane had drifted to. Unfortunately a rope became entangled in the propeller of the *Magpie*, so all her crew could do was to stand and watch as the *Tweedledum & Tweedledee* floated back down river towards the bridge.

Once again the bridge was hit, the floating crane hitting hard the dolphins on pier twenty, with the jib of the crane striking the underside of the bridge. This caused another £6,000 worth of damage to the bridge as well as serious damage to herself, requiring a spell at Avonmouth Docks for repair. Back on station at the bridge, new moorings for the *Tweedledum & Tweedledee* had been devised to prevent another serious disaster happening. Fortunately this part of the contract was coming to end, although it would still be some time before any definite decision was made on the future of the bridge.

Following the Severn Bridge Disaster of Tuesday, 25th October 1960 companies wanted compensation for damage to the bridge, loss of material and other costs. The case between John Harker Ltd and the British Transport Commission began in the courts during 1961. Others came to the court to make their claim, the Fairfield Shipbuilding & Engineering Co Ltd, South West Gas Board and the Postmaster General. Fairfield's claim was for £8,704-10s-8d but when the proceedings ended all they were awarded was a little over £100, with British Rail getting an award of £5,000.

Each year discussions took place of what the future of the bridge would be, many options being discussed. In 1965 the army was invited to the bridge to discuss a project of them demolishing the bridge. Plans of the bridge was looked at in great detail by the army but any thoughts of them carrying out a military exercise in demolition were dropped for various reasons.

That same year twenty-four companies were asked to submit a tender for the demolition of the bridge among them Underwater Welders Ltd of Cardiff and a local Sharpness company, I.P.L. Shipyards. A site meeting had been arranged for the 3rd and 4th March to allow these companies a chance to see for themselves what the demolition job entailed. After this visit twenty of the twenty-four companies withdrew

Demolition of the Severn Railway Bridge in 1967 with the redundant Aust ferry, SEVERN KING assisting

their bids!

The company who finally won the contract was Nordman Construction Company Limited of Gloucester. Although not one of the original twenty-four companies asked to tender, their tender when accepted, was the lowest.

During 1967 Nordman Construction announced to the press that demolition would be starting soon and that a huge floating crane from Hamburg, the *Magnus II*, would be used on the project. The *Magnus II* arrived on Tuesday 22nd August at 9.30am, piloted up the Severn estuary by a local man, Doug Griffey of Sharpness. This huge floating crane was considered to be the best there was, with a lifting capacity of 400 tons to a height of 150 feet, self-propelled with four propellers, one on each corner of the hull and ballast tanks to ensure she kept on an even keel. The cost to hire though, was expensive, over a £1,000 per day, thus the demolition company made plans to get the most work out of her in as less time as possible.

Their plans went terribly wrong. The *Magnus II* worked in the river from the 23rd August until she left on the 11th September, at a total cost of £21,000 and she left behind twenty-one piers, three spans and the swing bridge still standing in the river!

All was not well, Nordman Construction were getting behind with the planned time schedule of the demolition of the bridge and viaduct, giving cause for concern to the district civil engineer. He demanded an explanation from the demolition company why the viaduct would not be demolished by Sunday 31st December.

It was agreed that the viaduct would have to be blown up and Swinnerton & Miller Ltd of Willenhall were sub-contracted to do the job. On Sunday 10th March 1968, not quite three months after the original deadline for the demolition of the viaduct, explosives had been placed in the stonework. The whole operation had been treated as top secret and at 7.30am, under the glare of floodlights the silence was broken by the first blast. Finally the viaduct was gone, just a mass of rubble and stone lying in the mud.

Demolition work had been going on for eight months; with no sign of the slick operation planned by Nordman Construction Company Limited and still no end in sight of when the bridge would be finally demolished. To add to their worries a request for £30,000 as an interim payment was refused. Then it was learned that Ulrich Harms, owner of the floating crane, *Magnus II*, was taking them to court for non payment of their bill.

Eventually the receivers were called in to decide that Nordman Construction Company Limited would go into liquidation and take no further part in the demolition of the bridge. This left British Railways the problem of finding another company willing to carry on with the demolition of the bridge.

Swinnerton & Miller agreed terms to carry on with the demolition and used the ex Beachley to Aust ferryboat, *Severn King*, to help with the operation. A crane had been placed on the vessel's deck turntable and this proved useful in lifting steel from the river into waiting barges. On the night of Friday 4th July 1969 disaster was to strike again. The *Severn King* broke adrift on a large tide and became impaled on the stump of pier number two. At low water the damage was excessive, a large hole in the hull and with the tides dropping it meant that there was no chance of floating her off the pier, so temporary repairs were made to the hull before awaiting a suitable tide in which to float her off. On the evening of Monday 28th July the *Severn King* was re-floated and towed to the shore by Sharpness Piers and subsequently scrapped.

The end was finally in sight, for on Sunday 25th January 1970 the last remaining part of the Severn Railway Bridge were removed. An elegant bridge with a history unmatched by any other that crosses the Severn. It is sad that this bridge is only remembered for tragedy and not the joy it gave many people as they travelled over it on the train with a wonderful view of the river far below.

The magnificent Severn Railway Bridge showing the swing bridge over the Gloucester & Sharpness Ship Canal

Looking towards the bow of both vessels (WASTDALE H is on the left).
Firemen had the difficult job of gaining access to the WASTDALE H

Captain George Thompson (1927 - 2007)

George Thompson was born in 1927 in the small Yorkshire town of Maltby. On leaving school at fourteen years of age he went to work down the pits. One of his passion's during this period was amateur boxing and he gained a reputation as being a good fighter.

Soon after the outbreak of war he had no choice but to sign on as a Bevan Boy, something he hated and as soon as the war ended, he was out of the pits and finding work elsewhere.

In 1949 he found himself working at Gloucester at a local laundry. This was not to last and George decided to do something entirely different, working as a deckhand on one of John Harker's tanker barges on the River Severn! It was not long before he had worked his way up to mate on the large vessels trading down to Swansea.

It was while mate on the WIDDALE H that he had his first disaster. Loaded with petrol bound for Worcester the vessel was going through the narrow channel of the Nash at Llantwit Major on 1st April 1959 on an ebbing tide. The WIDDALE H touched bottom and in poor visibility became stuck!

Then between tides the wind increased to gale force and lifted the vessel onto the rocks. The cargo tanks were holed and the crew became trapped aft with petrol washing over them. The Fire Brigade attended and the crew was hauled to safety up the face of the cliff.

George remained with Harker's until the early 1970s, then he left to become skipper of sand dredgers working in the Bristol Channel. Before retiring from the sea he delivered two old sand dredgers, the HARRY BROWN and the SAND SAPPHIRE to Bahrain.

At the latter end of his life he stood in the local elections and became elected as a Councillor with Gloucester City Council.

George Thompson on the deck of the ROSEDALE H in Newport Docks.

The WIDDALE H loaded at Swansea.

44

More Disasters

The Severn Railway Bridge had been hit before when on 4th February 1939 three small tanker barges got into difficulty off Sharpness. The SEVERN TRAVELLER was towing two barges when the tow-rope parted as they swung off Sharpness. Soon all three vessels were swept in to the bridge and capsized. That night six men lost their lives as a result of the accident.

The capsized SEVERN CARRIER off Purton.

On the 16th February 1961 the loaded tanker barge BP EXPLORER entered the Severn Estuary on the evening tide bound for Sharpness. The following morning a watchman on the damaged Severn Railway Bridge heard a loud thump and was shocked to see the upturned hull of the BP EXPLORER bouncing her way through the bridge. The vessel had turned over on the previous night tide and all five crew men were killed.

The Fire Service looking for missing crew members, (left) and, (below) men working on salvaging the BP EXPLORER.

The vessel was eventually rebuilt and renamed BP DRIVER but a few months later on a trip to Swansea she was driven ashore in a gale off Llantwit Major.

45

Epilogue

Of the three surviving crew members only Capt. George Thompson continued working for John Harker Ltd. The WYESDALE H was rebuilt in 1961 to allow this vessel to trade down to Swansea and a new skipper, mate and engineer were appointed. In fact only the lad, Chris Witts, remained as part of the original crew.

George Thompson became skipper, Mike Edwards the mate and with Chris the three of them remained together for several years. Life was never boring trading to all the Bristol Channel ports and then going far inland to Worcester. Accidents continued to happen and indeed the WYESDALE H was involved in a fatal tragedy when the vessel hit a rescue launch at the new Severn Suspension Bridge in November 1961.

Soon after the Severn Bridge Disaster the two wrecks were sold for a nominal sum to a local contractor. It is his opinion that if the army had not blown holes in the hulls then there was a possibility that they could have been salvaged. Apparently, considering the severity of the fire, the two barges suffered very little fire damage!

Chris Witts as a deckhand on the WYESDALE H at 16 yrs of age.

Skipper George Thompson posing on the deck of the WYESDALE H in 1961.

© Ted Witts

Rough seas on the ROSEDALE H off Llantwit Major in 1962

Finally, in 1963, all three of them joined the new vessel WINSDALE H